A Man After God's Own Heart

A Man After God's Own Heart

Based on the Life of David

Brad Stewart and Brian Doyle

Scripture quotations taken from the New American Standard Bible®, Copyright © 1960, 1962, 1963, 1968, 1971, 1972, 1973, 1975, 1977, 1995 by The Lockman Foundation

Used by permission. (www.Lockman.org)

Cover Design by DeeDee Heathman
Interior Design by DeeDee Heathman
Library of Congress Cataloging-in-Publication Data

Stewart, Brad and Doyle, Brian
    A Man After God's Own Heart: Based on the Life of David
    p.cm.

ISBN: 978-1-61339-791-6
LCCN: 2015933795

1. RELIGION / Biblical Studies / Old Testament
2. RELIGION / Christian Life / Men's Issues
3. RELIGION / Christian Life / Spiritual Growth

First Edition
Printed in the United States of America

To contact Iron Sharpens Iron go to: www.IronSharpensIron.net
For further information contact Made for Success Publishing,
+1 425 526 6480 or email at Service@madeforsuccess.net

Dedication

To all those who have co-labored with men in the harvest fields of men's souls, we want to thank you for being godly, masculine men. Men who are not afraid to act with boldness on one hand yet be as gentle as a lamb on the other. Men who see the value in studying God's Holy Word and inactively engaging with God through the Bible. May your tribe increase!

TABLE OF CONTENTS

PREFACE

From Brad

During my tour of active duty in the US military, one of my close friends shared a few insights from a book on the life of David by AW Pink. It pricked my interest then and continues to influence my thinking today. This study is a result from continued learning and meditation on this fascinating man of God.

Next to Jesus, the Scriptures cover more of David's life than any other man. David, Israel's greatest king, is one of the most amazing men who ever lived. He is known as being a man after God's own heart (1 Samuel 13:14; Acts 13:22), yet his life is filled with similar ups and downs as those faced by most men today. In some situations, he displays deep faith and trust in God—while, other times, he sounds depressed and discouraged. In other situations, he makes horrible decisions that impact his family, his work, and his community. Through all of his ups and downs, he still maintains his faith. Consequently, there are things in David's life which we should emulate, and things which we should avoid. Therein lies the hope for God's men today.

This Bible study was developed to help you study the Scriptures, discover the greatness and weakness of this king, and make applications so you can emulate the godly parts of David's life and avoid the harsh consequences of disobedience.

From Brian

It is unique in the scriptures that we have the opportunity to get to know a character as well as we get to know David. Starting in chapter 16 of I Samuel and through II Samuel and even in I Kings, we see the life of David. From chapter 11 of I Chronicles to the end in chapter 29, we read his story with different details. Approximately half the Book of Psalms is written by David, and much of this corresponds with the events of his life. The life and works and writings of Solomon remind us of David as well. The quantity of text helps us see this man from his early days as a young son of Jesse to his final days as a father giving a charge to his own son.

The quantity of his story is helpful, but it is the quality of the story that draws us to David. The scriptures give us access to private conversations and some of David's inner most thoughts. We become acquainted with feats of bravery as well as moments of cowardice. We see a man who is tender and compassionate with others as well as the warrior who is ruthless against his enemies. The same man who passionately loves his God also has moments of denial and disconnect. The father and husband who is emotionally invested in his family is also the same man who abdicates his responsibilities, resulting in significant dysfunction in his family and a questionable legacy.

All of this helps us relate to David and embrace him in many ways as a man we might follow. Who does not want to follow a charismatic leader that is fueled by genuine passion to serve the Living God? We each understand, like David, what it is like to have sweet moments of success and sour moments of personal failure. The honesty and transparency of the scriptures makes a Bible study on the life of David so compelling. We study and digest true stories of a man who has gone before us. This bible study is designed to engage you with God and His Spirit through the story of a man He selected to follow Him and lead His people.

Studying the life of David will be a blessing to both men and women, old and young, mature or new in their faith. This imperfect man gives hope to the one who desires to follow and know the same One True God. The

PREFACE

Apostle Paul, in his travels as a leader of the emerging Christian Church, references in Acts 13 how Samuel rebuked Saul and informed him that God had raised up a man after his own heart. This study is designed to point you in that same direction. It is our prayer that your heart, and not just your head, would turn to Almighty God as a result of your study.

INTRODUCTION

If you want to learn more about King David and becoming a man after God's own heart, then this Bible study is for you. It contains eight lessons that span the years of David's life until the day of his death and emphasizes personal application of biblical truth. By using an inductive study format, the Life of David enables you to discover for yourself what David did and how he sought after God. It is a fascinating study.

The eight lessons are divided into four sections. The first two lessons take place during his early years while he is emerging as a man and rising to the throne. The third and fourth lessons take place when David is an outlaw and pioneering his way through life. The fifth and sixth topics happen during his reign as king while he is working full throttle in life and ministry. The last two lessons wrap up his story as a seasoned man who looks back on the years he has lived and the work God has done through his life. Together, these topics provide a nice overview of this amazing man, warrior, poet, father, and king.

While the overall content in this Bible study is designed for men, it can be useful for men and women alike in personal study or in a small group situation. No matter if you are young in the faith, a mature man, or a woman, there is something for everyone in this fascinating biblical account. He is a man after God's own heart (Acts 13:22).

"Make me know Your ways, O LORD; Teach me Your paths.

Lead me in Your truth and teach me, For You are the God of my salvation; For You I wait all the day" (King David, in Psalm 25:4-5).

OVERVIEW OF DAVID'S LIFE

Saul was the first king of Israel, but he disobeyed God and God rejected Him. The decline of Saul and the rise of David are two of the most influential character studies that God's men should evaluate for lifetime applications. Their stories in Scripture contain timeless lessons and practical principles. Every man of God should read and consider these models and the eternal truths learned from their lives.

Saul is a man whose heart is divided between obeying God and putting himself first. Early in his reign, he is instructed to attack the Amalekites and totally destroy everything that belongs to them. Furthermore, he is not to spare anything including men, women, children, infants, cattle, sheep, camels, and donkeys. When he sees how well-fed and healthy the Amalekites keep their sheep and cattle, he spares the best and the fattest to use for worship sacrifices. To build up his own image, he puts a captured king on public exhibition. Next, to promote himself in the eyes of all Israel, he goes to Carmel and sets up a monument in his own honor. Clearly Saul is filled with pride and arrogance. After repeatedly disobeying God, he is rejected as king. God then chose the young shepherd David to take Saul's place. Most scholars divide David's life into three main sections.

Part I – A Man After God's Own Heart

As a young man, David tended his father's sheep in the wilderness. During these formative years, God molded his character and helped him develop several life skills as a shepherd. Besides shepherding skills, David learns to play a harp, compose Psalms of worship, grow physically and hit what he aims at with a sling. Throughout these early years, the young shepherd experiences a growing sense of dependence on God as he engages in a life struggle with wild animals seeking to devour the sheep in his father's flocks. After God rejects Saul, He assigns Samuel to visit the home of Jesse and anoint one of his sons who is a man after God's own heart. Unknown to Saul, he drafts David the future king into his service. Not having any state experience, David learns the basics for administrating a kingdom as a future king. Growing in his responsibilities and skills, David's success as a soldier thrust him into the national spotlight. The increased glory and attention David receives set off a spirit of envy and jealousy that results in repeated attempts to take David's life. As a fugitive on the run from a murderous leader, David learns to wait on God's timing. Eventually death comes to Saul and his sons while they are in battle against the Philistines. The people crown David as king of Judah fifteen years after his anointing.

Part II – A Man After God's Righteousness

David's early reign reveals military victories and national triumphs. After seven more years, his kingdom expands to include sovereignty over all Israel. As king, he sets up Jerusalem as the capital city and tries to bring the Ark of the Covenant back into its proper place. Eager to promote God's name, David seeks God's blessing to build a temple in the heart of Jerusalem. However, for God, David shed too much blood. God gives David a greater promise that from his line, his kingdom will never end. His continued triumphs come to an end when he is captivated by the beauty of a bathing woman, commits adultery, and then attempts to cover up his sin by manipulating her husband. When this fails, he has him murdered in battle. Nathan the prophet confronts David with his sin, and our fallen hero repents.

Part III – A Man After God's Reward

David's later reign reveals deep sins and personal tragedy. Although David repents and God forgives him, he reaps the effects of his actions for the rest of his life. Even with forgiveness, there are serious consequences to sin. In his resulting years, he experiences family strife, incest, murder, and rebellion. One son fakes an illness so he can take advantage of his attractive half-sister. When this fails, he rapes her. Another son undermines David's authority and leads a coup to overthrow his father and take control of all Israel. During his later years as king, David forgets where the true power of life comes from and numbers the fighting men in the military. Sadly, as an old man he is impotent and broken.

Conclusion

David experiences highs and lows in life, just like every man. In the end, he realized that God was in his everyday world affecting his everyday circumstances. Like David, *all men* should make everyday life central in their thinking about God. Unlike David, all men should consider the outcomes of their behavior before they choose a course of action which impacts God's name, those they love, and those they lead. David is a model of repentant faith whose failures are forgiven and whose accomplishments are the result of God's purpose.

Map of Israel During the Life of David

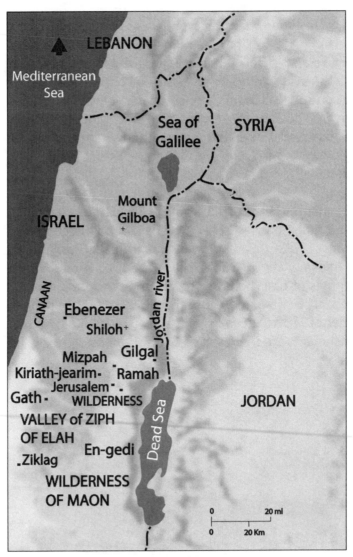

Map During the life of David

The broken lines (– • – •) indicate modern boundaries.

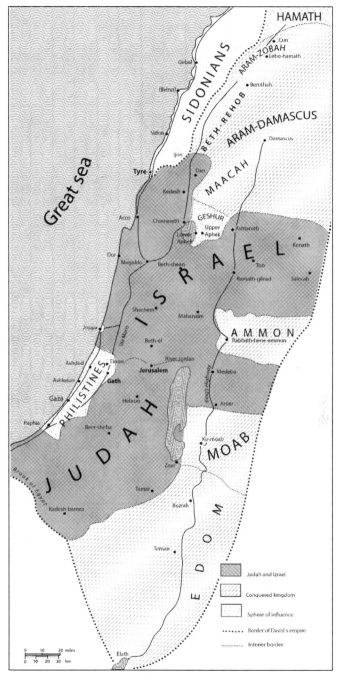

The Kingdom of David

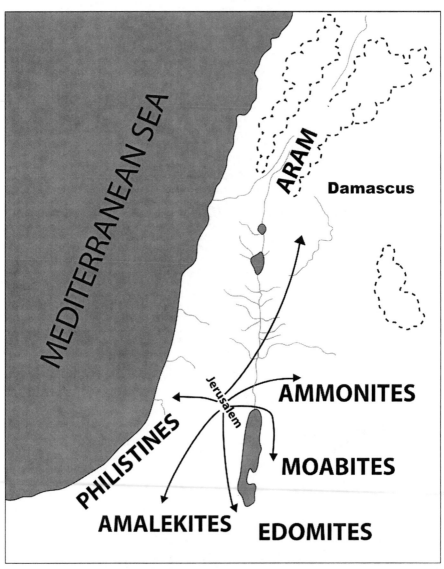

Map of Nations Conquered by David

1

The Battle Belongs to the Lord

1 Samuel 17:1 – 31

S aul's army is facing battle with the Philistines championed by a giant named Goliath. Goliath taunts the army of God—especially its fearful king. While on a trip to supply provisions for his brothers, David hears the giant rant his defiance of Israel's army, God, and king. In an act of bravery and courage, young David uses his skills, exercises his faith, and then cuts off Goliath's head. Israel defeats the enemy, and Saul recognizes David.

I. Battle Lines – 1 Samuel 17:1-31

    A. Describe the enemy and their forces for battle. (vv 1-11)

DID YOU KNOW?

The ancient Greeks, to whom the Philistines were apparently related, sometimes decided issues of war through chosen champions who met in combat between the armies. Through this economy of warriors, the judgment of the gods on the matter at stake was determined.... Israel too may have known this practice. (1 Sam. 17:4, 2 Sam. 2 14-16)[2]

B. What did you learn about David as a young man? (vv 12-27)

C. How does David react to his brother's criticism? (vv 28-30)

D. Do you have memories of family members giving you criticism or unsolicited feedback?

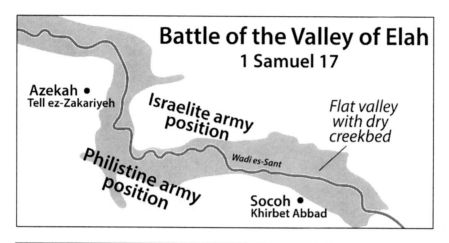

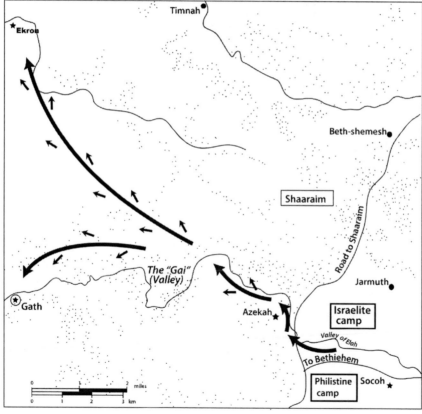

The Valley of Elah

II. Battle Courage – 1 Samuel 17:32-39

    A. Describe the dialogue between David and King Saul (vv 31-33).

    B. What experiences in life did God sovereignly provide so he would have the skills and confidence to face a giant warrior like Goliath? (vv 34-37)

    C. In what ways has this principle been true in your own life?

    D. Although David was an expert at protecting sheep, whom did he rely on? (v 37)

E. Why did Saul dress David in his tunic and coat of arms? (vv 38-39) What was the condition of Saul's faith in God?

III. Battle Tactics – 1 Samuel 17:40-58

A. How did David prepare for the battle? (v 37-40)

DID YOU KNOW?

"Usually the stones chosen were round and smooth and somewhat larger than a baseball. When hurled by a master slinger, they probably traveled at close to 100 miles per hour." David picked up five stones. Some theologians believe he armed himself with five stones because Goliath had four giant relatives. Others believe he was being prudent in case of increased attacks or needing to rearm and continue the warfare. (1 Sam. 17:40, 2 Sam. 21: 19-22)[3]

B. What was Goliath's reaction to doing battle with David? (vv 41-44)

C. How does David's response demonstrate his faith and willingness to face Goliath ? (vv 45-47)

D. Describe the battle and David's actions. (vv 48-54)

E. Can you identify a time in your life when you wanted to challenge someone because they dishonored the Name of the Lord?

F. What are Saul's feelings toward David after killing Goliath? (vv 55-58)

G. In the 21st century, how should Christians stand firm or march forward against the Goliaths of this world?

DISCIPLESHIP PRINCIPLE

Have you ever been marginalized by someone? Or perhaps you allowed the criticism of others to stop you from moving forward and facing a difficult situation. Goliath sized up David and concluded he was not fit for combat. With God, one is a majority.

While this warfare on earth was between a young man and warrior giant, the real battle was between the God of Israel and the pagan god of the Philistines. Throughout the Bible, God moves in dramatic ways to make His sovereign power known both to Israel and to the nations of the world. Most of the men watching this battle saw a huge fierce warrior. David saw a mere man who was defying the army of the living God. He knew when he faced Goliath he was not alone. Through his experience in the fields he acquired battle skills and faith for this moment. He knew he was not alone, the Lord would fight with him. Sometimes we forget to look at the Goliaths in our life using a God perspective. Viewing difficult or impossible situations from God's perspective keeps them in a biblical perception. What is one giant in your life right now? How can you exercise your faith in facing it?

Personal Application:

BATTLES BELONG TO THE LORD

To help keep this perspective, take some time during the week to meditate on and memorize the Scripture below.

Scripture Memory and Meditation Verse

Battles Belong to the Lord – 1 Sam 17:47

"And that all this assembly may know that the LORD does not deliver by sword or by spear; for the battle is the LORD'S and He will give you into our hands."

For the battle is the
LORD'S
AND HE WILL GIVE YOU
INTO OUR HANDS

2

Friendship, Envy, and Jealousy

1 Samuel 18:1 – 19:24

As David grows in his roles, responsibilities and relationships, Saul grows in envy and jealousy. In a plot to kill young David, Saul offers his daughters in marriage. Instead of dying, David doubles the needed dowry and foils the plot. Saul's hatred grows while David's fame spreads. Caught in the middle, Jonathon tries to honor his father, and to love David as a brother. After another fit of rage from King Saul, David seeks help from Samuel the prophet. Saul seeks to find and kill David, but in a strange act of God's Spirit, God protects David.

I. Growing Friendship – 1 Samuel 18:1-4

    A. What are five characteristics that you find in the relationship between David and Jonathon? (vv 1-4)

DID YOU KNOW?

The word covenant occurs 301 times in the ESV Bible. It is an arrangement between two parties involving mutual obligations; especially the arrangement that established the relationship between God and his people, expressed in grace first with Israel and then with the church. The essence of covenant is found in a particular kind of relationship between persons. Thus a covenant relationship is not merely a mutual acquaintance but a commitment to responsibility and action. A key word in Scripture to describe that commitment is "faithfulness," acted out in a context of abiding friendship. (1 Sam. 18:3)[4]

B. What does it mean to make a covenant with another man or to have a man who is closer than a brother? (See Proverbs 18:24.)

C. You may have had a friend like this in the past, but do you presently have a 'friend who sticks closer than a brother'? If so, who is he? If not, are there any potential close friends for you to develop?

II. Rising Envy and Increasing Glory – 1 Samuel 18:5-30

    A. In what ways did David grow in success? (vv 5-7)

    B. How did Saul react to David's rising success and glory? (vv 8-9).

    C. Describe the contrast between Saul and David. (vv 10-16)

    D. Why did the Spirit of the Lord depart from Saul? (vv 16:14)

E. What does Saul devise as a means of getting rid of David? (vv 17-30)

III. Reconciling Relationships – 1 Samuel 19:1-10

A. Describe Jonathon's attempt to restore David and Saul's relationship. (vv 1-7)

B. What happens as a result? (vv 7-10)

IV. Surviving Hatred – 1 Samuel 19:11-24

    A. Describe the situation for David and Michal. How do you think this influenced their marriage? (vv 11-17)

    B. If you are married, have you experienced meddling from parents and in-laws?

    C. If you have children that are married, in what ways do you guard yourself from this?

    D. How did Saul react to this? (vv 18-22)

E. In what way does God intervene on David's behalf? (vv 23-24)

DID YOU KNOW?

During the time of Kings, schools existed for training the prophets. Most likely Samuel was training these men for the future ministry. Some Jewish writers think these messengers prophesied the advancement of David to the throne of Israel.[5] Regardless of the message, they all were overpowered by the presence of God. (1 Sam. 19:23-24)

F. What is one situation right now that you need Almighty God to intervene on your behalf?

Eventually, every disciple faces having to choose a course of action because two people closely related to him make opposing demands. When obedience to parents becomes opposed to the bonds of love and friendship, one relationship must be sacrificed for the other. In a similar way, when obedience to God becomes opposed to the bonds of love and friendship with others, the relationship with Christ must take precedence.

Psalm 59 was written during this period in David's life. Take a few minutes to read through Psalm 59. All of us have struggles—sometimes with family, sometimes with friends, and sometimes with enemies. Regardless of who you struggle with, God wants His men to rely on Him (Psalm 59:16-17). Has God delivered you from struggles at work in the past? Are you currently struggling in any personal relationships? Have you ever been wounded or betrayed? What are some ways you can lean into God and trust Him for a resolution?

Personal Application:

GOD'S PROTECTION

To help keep this perspective, take some time during the week to meditate on and memorize the Scripture below.

Scripture Memory and Meditation Verse

God's Protection – Psalm 59:1-2

"Deliver me from my enemies, O my God; Set me securely on high away from those who rise up against me. Deliver me from those who do iniquity and save me from men of bloodshed."

Regardless of who you struggle with,
GOD
WANTS HIS MEN TO RELY ON HIM

3

Trusting Self

1 Samuel 21:1-15

Up to now, David has followed the Lord's design for his life. In fact, he has been a model of a good man; humble, faithful, and honest. Suddenly, God puts his faith to the test. His life is in danger; his best friend is put into a situation where he must choose between friendship and obedience to his father, and his wife acts to honor her father while saving her husband. Like so many men today, David reacts to the situation by taking things into his own hands. His actions and words bring about dire results for others.

I. Lies to Ahimelech – 1 Samuel 21:1-9

    A. How does the priest Ahimelech greet David? (v 1)

    B. David lies to Ahimelech (vv 2-6). When is it permissible to tell a lie?

DID YOU KNOW?

"The bread of the Presence" (see Exodus 25: 30; Leviticus 24: 5-9; 1 Samuel 21: 6) or "shew bread" (KJV) was twelve loaves that were placed each week in the Holy Place of the tabernacle. They were a thank offering for the provision of daily bread, consecrating the fruit of Israel's labors. "Presence" refers to God's presence as provider and Lord. When the week-old loaves were replaced with fresh ones, only the priests could eat them. Ahimelech stretched the law to let David's men have them if the men were ceremonially clean by abstaining from sex (see Exodus 19: 15; Leviticus 15: 18).[6]

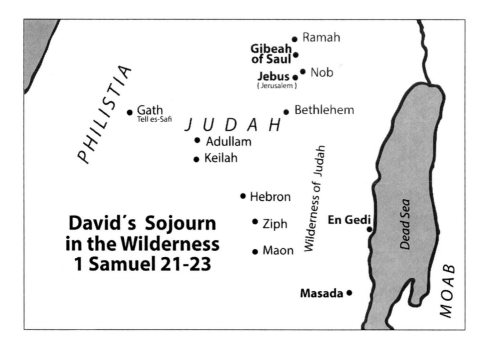

David's Sojourn in the Wilderness
1 Samuel 21-23

C. What is significant about Doeg the Edomite? (v 7)

D. Is it wrong in times of trouble to manipulate our situation? (v 8) Why or why not?

E. How important was the sword of Goliath? (v 9)

II. Lies to Achish – 1 Samuel 21:10-15

   A. What is significant about the area of Gath? (v 10)
      (See 1 Samuel 17:4.)

DID YOU KNOW?

Gath was a walled city and one of the five chief cities of the Philistines, which also included Gaza, Ashdod, Ashkelon, and Ekron, all situated on or near the southern coast of Palestine. Although frequently involved in conflict with the Israelites, the city was apparently not subdued until David's time. It was a Canaanite city, the home of the giant Goliath and other men of great height. A remnant of the Anakim was left, even after the extensive campaigns of Joshua (1 Sam.6:17, 17:4, 21:10, 2 Sam 21:18-22, 2 Cor. 26:6, Jos 10:36-39, 11:21-22, 13:3, 1 Cor. 18:1)[7]

   B. How did the people of Gath view David? (v 11)

C. What was David's reaction? (v 12)

D. Why did he act like a madman? (v 13)

E. David is desperate. He is out of control. Has there been a time in your life when you felt this type of desperation?

F. How does Achish view the situation? (v 14)

DISCIPLESHIP PRINCIPLE

God clearly wants His men to lean on Him in times of difficulty. If a man is too dependent on family, friends, or his talents, God will take him through a set of circumstances that result in removing any crutch. Taking things into our own hands and telling lies to protect ourselves is not leaning on God. He is the only source of faith and salvation from our troubles in life.

Through this turbulent and difficult time in his life, David learned to depend on God. As part of how he processed his experience with God, he wrote Psalm 56 to reflect when the Philistines seized him in Gath. He wrote Psalm 34 to express what he learned when he feigned madness before Achish. What are the turbulent things you are facing? How can David's story and Psalms help you grow in experiencing God?

Personal Application:

SEEK THE LORD

To help keep this perspective, take some time during the week to meditate on and memorize the Scripture below.

Scripture Memory and Meditation Verse

Seek the Lord – Psalm 34:9-10

"O fear the LORD, you His saints; for to those who fear Him there is no want. The young lions do lack and suffer hunger; but they who seek the LORD shall not be in want of any good thing."

God is the only
SOURCE OF FAITH
AND SALVATION
FOR OUR TROUBLES IN LIFE.

4

Turmoil and Tragedy

1 Samuel 22:1-23

Filled with despair, David finds refuge in the cave at Adullam. Here he begins to seek out the help of God and the comfort of family and friends. No doubt, his aging parents were not able to keep pace with him and his men. After finding refuge for his parents in the land of their ancestry, he continues to stay on the move. Meanwhile, Saul, filled with murderous hatred, commands the genocide of eighty-five men of God, their families, and their livestock.

I. The Cave – 1 Samuel 22:1-5

    A. What is the condition of David's heart while in the cave? (v 1) (See Psalm 142.)

    B. What do you think happened to cause David's desperation to now push him toward God?

DID YOU KNOW?

The Cave of Adullam has been discovered about 2 miles south of the scene of David's triumph, and about 13 miles west from Bethlehem. At this place is a hill some 500 feet high pierced with numerous caverns, in one of which David gathered together "every one that was in distress, and every one that was in debt, and every one that was discontented" (1 Sam. 22:2). Some of these caverns are large enough to hold 200 or 300 men. (1 Sam. 22:1)[8]

C. Describe the kind of men who were becoming part of his band of brothers. (v 2)

D. Why was it important for David to find safe refuge for his parents? (vv 3-5)

E. Can you think of a reason, based on his ancestry, why he may have felt positive about making this request of the King of Moab? (See Ruth 1:4, 4:13-22.)

II. The Consequence – 1 Samuel 22:6-19

    A. In what way does Saul motivate his men to seek David's life? (vv 6-8)

    B. What is the family background of Doeg the Edomite? (vv 9-10) (See Genesis 25:30.)

    C. Why did Saul seek the audience of Ahimelech and his entire family? (vv 11-13)

    D. How does Ahimelech respond to Saul's accusations? (vv 14-15)

    E. What is the reaction of the guards to Saul's execution order? What does this say about the posture of Saul with his men? (vv 16-19)

    F. Has there been a time recently when you have searched your conscience and have needed to say no to an authority?

G. Why is Doeg the Edomite so willing to kill God's anointed? (vv 18-19)

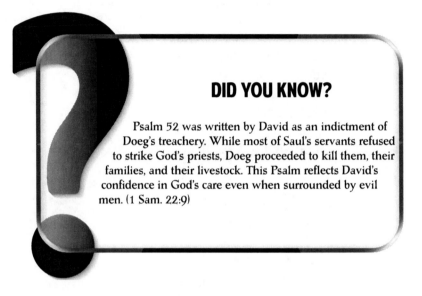

DID YOU KNOW?

Psalm 52 was written by David as an indictment of Doeg's treachery. While most of Saul's servants refused to strike God's priests, Doeg proceeded to kill them, their families, and their livestock. This Psalm reflects David's confidence in God's care even when surrounded by evil men. (1 Sam. 22:9)

III. The Concern – 1 Samuel 22:20-23

A. What happens to **Abiathar** in the aftermath of his family's execution? (vv 20-23)

B. How does David react to the news? (See Psalm 52.)

DISCIPLESHIP PRINCIPLE

Part of David's preparation to reign is seeking and trusting in the leadership and care of God. God wants His men to trust fully in His sovereign control. The Lord often takes men through great periods of turmoil and tragedy in preparation for their future. Are you facing a situation where your life is in turmoil?

David's response to these situations in his life are captured in Psalm 142 and 52. He wrote Psalm 142 during his time in the cave. In this Psalm, David laments over his hopeless situation.

The life of David and the life of Christ reflect the lives of two leaders who worked with men in ways that transformed lives. David took men who were distressed, in debt, and bitter and turned them into a mighty, army. Jesus took fisherman, zealots, and tax collectors and turned them into kingdom builders that changed the world. Both of them took ordinary men and trained them to live extra-ordinary lives.

Do the examples of David and Jesus challenge your thinking as it relates to developing as a man or as an effective man in a team of men?

Personal Application:

CRY OUT TO GOD

To help keep this perspective, take some time during the week to meditate on and memorize the Scripture below.

Scripture Memory and Meditation

Cry Out to God – Psalm 142:1-2

"I cry aloud with my voice to the LORD; I make supplication with my voice to the LORD. I pour out my complaint before Him; I declare my trouble before Him."

The Lord often takes men through GREAT PERIODS OF TURMOIL AND TRAGEDY IN PREPARATION FOR THEIR FUTURE.

5

The Presence and Providence of God

Psalm 139:1

David wrote Psalm 139 as praise to God for His knowledge of all things, His presence throughout the universe, and His foresight over the earth. He understood that God wants all of His people to fear acts of sin, walk in holiness, and live as intentional believers. In His care and concern for His people, God knows everything and still loves those who are children in His family. The Psalm begins and ends with a prayerful request for God to search David's heart. This is a great example for all of us to follow.

I. God's Knowledge – Psalm 139:1-6

    A. What were some of the things God knew about the life of David? (vv 1-4)

B. Does this knowledge that God has of you bring comfort? Does it bring anxiety? Describe the reasons why.

C. How did David see God's involvement in his life? (v 5)

D. What is the Psalmist's reaction to learning about God's knowledge of all things? (v 6)

II. God's Presence – Psalm 139:7-12

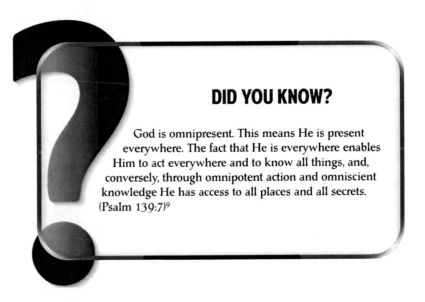

DID YOU KNOW?

God is omnipresent. This means He is present everywhere. The fact that He is everywhere enables Him to act everywhere and to know all things, and, conversely, through omnipotent action and omniscient knowledge He has access to all places and all secrets. (Psalm 139:7)[9]

A. Why are these two questions important for every man to consider? (v 7)

B. Where can a man hide from the presence of God? (vv 8-10)

C. Describe a situation where darkness or isolation may change the way you think. How can the darkness impact our thinking in regards to the presence of God? (vv 11-12)

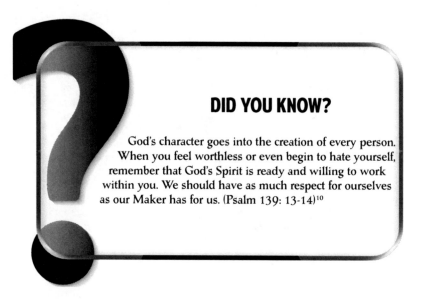

DID YOU KNOW?

God's character goes into the creation of every person. When you feel worthless or even begin to hate yourself, remember that God's Spirit is ready and willing to work within you. We should have as much respect for ourselves as our Maker has for us. (Psalm 139: 13-14)[10]

III. God's Providence – Psalm 139:13-18

A. What did David understand in regards to God's creative work in humans? (vv 13-14)

B. What is God's knowledge of His creatures before they are conceived? (vv 15-16)

C. How do these truths of scripture impact your personal convictions on the laws of the day?

D. Why is it important to recognize the providence of God? (v 16)

IV. God's Protection – Psalm 139:19-22

A. What are David's views about men who rejected the presence of God? (vv 19-22)

B. Should 21st century Christians hate those who hate God? (vv 21-22)

C. Why or why not?

V. Man's Response – Psalm 139:23-24

A. Why is it important for you to ask God to search your heart, test your thoughts, and be guided in ways that matter for eternity? (vv 23-24)

B. How important is it for a man to ask God to point out his sin?

C. When and where would this happen?

DISCIPLESHIP PRINCIPLE

Some men have a tendency to behave one way in a group but another way when they are alone. Almost all the great sins in a man's life are committed when he isolates himself. This is especially compounded when he is alone and dwells in spiritual darkness. Unfortunately, it is easier to dive into the pleasures of sin than it is to pursue sensing His presence and seeking first His righteousness. The more time you spend in His presence getting to know Him, the stronger you become; the stronger you, become the more of His light shines in your life. When was the last time you sat alone and sought the presence of God?

Other men sometimes view themselves as worthless beings or hate themselves. When these kinds of thoughts impact your mind, remember God's Spirit is prepared and eager to work within you. Men of God should have as much respect for themselves as the Lord does for His creation. Do you often feel insignificant or of no value?

Personal Application:

THE PRESENCE OF GOD

To help keep this perspective, take some time during the week to meditate on and memorize the Scripture below.

Scripture Memory and Meditation

The Presence of God Psalm 139:7-10

"Where can I go from Your Spirit? or where can I flee from Your presence? If I ascend to heaven, You are there; If I make my bed in Sheol, behold, You are there. If I take the wings of the dawn If I dwell in the remotest part of the sea, Even there Your hand will lead me, And Your right hand will lay hold of me."

Almost all the great sins
IN A MAN'S LIFE
ARE COMMITTED WHEN HE ISOLATES
HIMSELF.

6

The Danger of Lust

2 Samuel 11:1-27

When David should have been on the battlefield, he is lying in bed and indulging his flesh. Looking out from his rooftop, he finds the beauty of a bathing woman and gives in to his lust of the flesh. Not only does he yield to his lust, he carries his sin further by trying to cover up his actions through manipulation, intoxication, and murder.

I. Lust and Sexual Sin – 2 Samuel 11:1-5

    A. Where is David during the time for countries to wage war? (v 1)

DID YOU KNOW?

Winter is the rainy season in Israel, the time when crops are planted. Spring was a good time to go to war because the roads were dry, making travel easier for troop movements, supply wagons, and chariots. In Israel, wheat and barley were ready to be harvested in the spring. These crops were an important food source for traveling armies. (2 Sam. 11:1)[11]

B. How does David respond to seeing a beautiful naked woman? (vv 1-4)

C. Where in life are you in an authority position? In what role do you give orders that others obey? Have you recently misused your authority to get what you want? In what way?

D. What is the result for both of David and Bathsheeba? (v 5)

II. Manipulation and Control – 2 Samuel 11:6-13

    A. Why does David send for Uriah to return home? (v 6)

    B. What orders are given to Uriah? (vv 7-8)

    C. How does he react? (v 9)

    D. Why does Uriah refuse the king? (vv 10-11)

    E. In what ways do we see the desperation of David arise again in this specific scene? (vv 12-13)

    F. Uriah was a noble warrior. David's desperation and misuse of power ignored this man's right actions. Have you ever experienced a leader who seemingly treated you unfairly?

III. Murder and Conspiracy – 2 Samuel 11:14-27

    A. How does David plan to remove Uriah permanently? (v 14)

    B. What is Joab's role in this conspiracy? (vv 15-22)

    C. How does David respond to the news that Uriah is dead? (vv 23-27)

DID YOU KNOW?

Joab was King David's cousin. He was the Son of Zeruiah, the half sister of David, who, along with his brothers Abishai and Asahel, was well known for his military valor in Judah. According to 2 Samuel, Joab rose to prominence and distinguished himself at the battle of Gibeon when Saul's troops under Abner were vanquished (2 Sam. 2:8-32, 2:18, 11:14-17, 26:6, 1 Cor 2:16) [12]

DISCIPLESHIP PRINCIPLE

If David could have foreseen the outcome of his actions, he would have done a much better job of guarding his heart. When it comes to biblical truth, the Bible states the facts and draws out lessons from the lives of God's men for both good and bad. David was careless in allowing his eyes to wander and then yield to the lust of his flesh. All men must learn to control the lust of the flesh, lust of the eyes, and the boastful pride of life (1 John 2:15-16). Otherwise, their evil wants drag them away into a world of enticement. After a desire is ill conceived, it gives birth to sin; and sin, when it is full-grown, gives birth to death (James 1:14-15).

Confession of sin does not automatically prevent divine judgment. Do not be deceived: God is not mocked, for whatever one sows, that will he also reap. For the one who sows to his own flesh will from the flesh reap corruption, but the one who sows to the Spirit will from Sprit reap eternal life (Galatians 6:7-8). Are you struggling with lust or sowing seeds of the flesh? What can you do to keep you mind pure?

Personal Application:

REPENTANCE

To help keep this perspective, take some time during the week to meditate on and memorize the Scripture below.

Scripture Memory and Meditation

Repentance – Psalm 51:10-12

"Create in me a clean heart, O God, And renew a steadfast spirit within me. Do not cast me away from Your presence And do not take Your Holy Spirit from me. Restore to me the joy of Your salvation And sustain me with a willing spirit."

All men must learn to CONTROL THE LUST OF THE FLESH, LUST OF THE EYES, AND THE BOASTFUL PRIDE OF LIFE.

7

Final Words and Faithful Friends

2 Samuel 23:1-39

This study contains two sections. In the first section, David speaks about leading men, and in the second is a list of the mighty men he led. In the process of leading and loving those around him, David develops strong bonds with this band of brothers who were mighty in deeds and loyal in their friendship. These men were loyal to David because he was loyal to them. If you want to know what kind of person a leader is, look at the kind of people that they lead.

I. Final Words 2 Samuel 23:1-7

    A. What is an oracle? (v 1)

    B. Who inspired the Psalms written by David? (v 2)

C. Who is the most 'godly' leader that you have ever known, and why?

D. How does David define godly leadership? (vv 3-4)

DID YOU KNOW?

Authors of the Navpress bible study on Samuel make a great point on this section of Scripture. They write, "The kingdom is attractive because the King is attractive. And the King is attractive because we have seen so little of this kind of ruler. Where, from democracy to dictatorship, have we found a ruler so controlled by godly fear and personal righteousness that his tenure actually revives and renews his people?" (2 Sam. 23:2-4)[13]

E. Describe the contrast between a man of God and a worthless man? (vv 5-7)

II. Faithful Friends – 2 Samuel 23:8-39

A. Summarize the exploits of David's leadership team.

Name	Accomplishment?
Josheb-Basshebeth	v 8
Eleazar	vv 9-10
Shammah	vv 11-12
All three together	vv 13-17
Abishai	vv 18-19
Behaiah	vv 20-23
Asahel	v 24

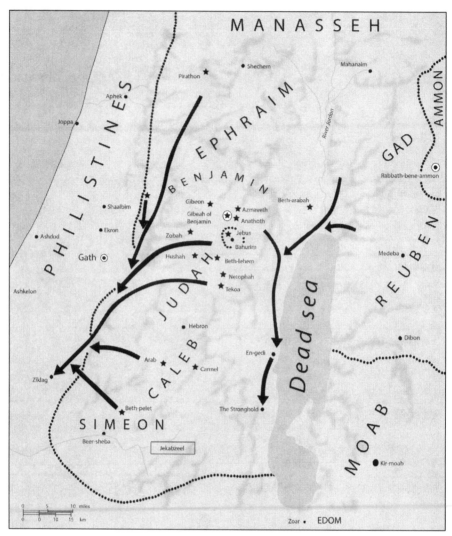

The Origins of David's Men

B. Why did David pour out his water as an offering to the Lord? (vv 16-17)

C. What is significant regarding Uriah the Hittie as the last in this list? (v 39)

D. If you could be one of David's Mighty Men who would you select? Why this man?

DID YOU KNOW?

There are *thirty-seven in all*: thirty-six names are mentioned in verses 8–39, so maybe Joab was the thirty-seventh. The *thirty* was a title rather than an exact figure, though it is likely that people who fell in battle were replaced, and we know that Asahel and Uriah died untimely deaths. All these men were renowned in their lifetimes and honoured by the king they served. (2 Sam. 2:23, 11:17, 23:8-39)[14]

DISCIPLESHIP PRINCIPLE

David was an outstanding leader when he was devoted to following His Leader. Devotion requires routine contact and submission. As we meet with God we can depend on Him for help and guidance. This fuels good leading and loving. Godly men who lead at home, at work, and in the community give life to others just like God gives life to them. As they live and love the people in their sphere of influence, their impact grows. Do you have godly close friends?

New Testament believers can look backward to David as they reflect on the life and ministry of Jesus. In the same way David trusted in the assurance of God's care and guidance, we can exercise our faith while living as brothers in the battles of life. God abided with David, and He abides with us (John 15). God promises to never leave us nor forsake us. And in a similar way as with David, He provides friendships for life.

When you die, what would you like to be remembered for?

Personal Application:

GODLY LEADERSHIP

To help keep this perspective, take some time during the week to meditate on and memorize the Scripture below

Scripture Memory and Meditation

Godly Leadership – 2 Samuel 23:3-4

"The God of Israel said, The Rock of Israel spoke to me, He who rules over men righteously, Who rules in the fear of God, Is as the light of the morning when the sun rises, A morning without clouds, When the tender grass springs out of the earth, Through sunshine after rain."

Godly men who lead at home, AT WORK, AND IN THE COMMUNITY GIVE LIFE TO OTHERS JUST LIKE GOD GIVES LIFE TO THEM.

8

On Your Death Bed

1 Kings 1:1-2:12

As David approaches seventy years of age, his body is weak and perhaps diseased. Adonijah sees this situation and attempts to set himself up as king. Sensing his inability to deal with more rebellions and to lead the kingdom, David declares Solomon as the next ruler of Israel. In a short but classic set of Scriptures, David the father issues Solomon the son a charge to be strong to show yourself a man by keeping the commandments of the Lord.

I. The Upward Rebellion – 1 Kings 1:1-27

    A. What is the condition of King David? (vv 1-4)

    B. What is one or more characteristics of David's fathering style that led to his family problems? (vv 5-6)

C. Who are those who joined with Adonijah and who are those who joined with David? (vv 7-10)

D. In your opinion, are there any surprises on whom joined forces with Adonijah? With David? (vv 11-27)

II. The Ultimate Ruler – 1 Kings 1:27-53

A. Describe the exchange between King David and Bathsheba? (v 28-37)

DID YOU KNOW?

The phrase, "As the Lord Lives" occurs thirty-five times in the ESV, and thirty-three of those occurrences are in the books of Samuel and Kings. The other two instances are in Judges and Ruth. The formal oath *As surely as the Lord* (Yahweh) *lives* is based on David's personal experience of divine deliverance (Heb. 'redeemed me', cf. 2 Sam. 4:9) and God's prior promise (2 Sam. 1:29, 4:13).[15]

B. What is unique in regards to having Solomon ride on David's mule? (v 38)

C. How did the people react to Solomon's coronation? (vv 39-40)

D. Why was it important for David to lavishly display his selection of Solomon? (vv 41-48)

E. How did Adonijah and the people with him react? (vv 49-53)

DID YOU KNOW?

Taking hold of the horns of the altar was a claim to protection, but it was not automatically guaranteed. In Exodus 21:12–14, the LORD said: "Anyone who strikes a man and kills him shall surely be put to death. However, if he does not do it intentionally, but God lets it happen, he is to flee to a place I will designate. If a man schemes and kills another man deliberately, take him away from my altar and put him to death." (1 Kings 1:50)[16]

III. The Ultra Challenge – 1 Kings 2:1-12

    A. Do you remember any charge that your own father gave to you? What was it? (vv 1-2)

    B. How does God reward those who live according to His word? (vv 3-4)

    C. What advice did David give his son regarding his enemies and friends? (vv 5-9)

    D. What is the condition of the kingdom, at the time of David's death? (vv 10-12)

DISCIPLESHIP PRINCIPLE

Like David to Solomon, all men should encourage and warn their sons be strong and to act like men. David gave sound advice to his son. It would be up to Solomon to follow it or not. All men need to use their strength and masculinity for the good of others. All men need to keep God the center of their personal and public life.

The Expositors Bible Commentary writes, "David's final words of admonition echo those of God to Joshua (Josh 1:6–9) as the latter was about to begin in his role as commander of the hosts of Israel (cf. also Deut 31:6–8, 23). The basic injunction was that Solomon should conduct himself in his personal life, and in his role as leader of God's people, in accordance with God's Word (cf. also Deut 17:18–20). Solomon was to be strong and show himself to be a man." [17] How much more important is it for us to encourage our sons and young men in the local church to be God's man in their home, workplace, and community.

Are you in a position to charge you own son(s) or other younger men that you influence?

Personal Application:

COMMAND YOUR SON

To help keep this perspective, take some time during the week to meditate on and memorize the Scripture below

Scripture Memory and Meditation

Command Your Son – 1 Kings 2:2-3a

"I am about to go the way of all the earth. Be strong, and show yourself a man, and keep the charge of the LORD your God, walking in his ways and keeping his statutes, his commandments, his rules, and his testimonies."

All men should ENCOURAGE AND WARN THEIR SONS TO BE STRONG AND TO ACT LIKE MEN.

FACILITATION GUIDE

The purpose of this section is to provide a basic framework for men's ministry Bible study discussions. Using this guide will help stimulate good discussion and mutual sharing among the men who participate in study group meetings. Being a good facilitator is not difficult; however, having a quality group discussion will take time, forethought, and effort. The more a facilitator works at improving his techniques, the more rewarding the content of his group discussions. *Keep in mind: it is all about the men across the table.*

For each session, the facilitator uses a set of questions to begin a discourse among the men in a group. The questions aim at getting the men feeling comfortable and lead into deeper conversation. Here is an example from a typical first session:

1. Be sure everyone in the group is introduced to one another
2. Q – Why did you choose to join a study like this one?
3. Q – What expectations do you personally have here at the beginning?
4. Q – What part of this study impressed you most?
5. Q – Why do feel that way?

During the discourse, there will be opportunities to help stimulate the conversation. Some men will need to be encouraged to open up and participate in the discussion; others will want to start conversing immediately. A major responsibility for a facilitator is to ensure that all men have an equal opportunity to participate and share.

Questions are a great way to stimulate and guide a group discussion. Kingdom Warrior and Iron Sharpens Iron Ministries recommend using five question types: approach, observation, interpretation, application, and extenders. Understanding how to use these types of questions enables a facilitator to guide, stimulate, and monitor the discussions of men. The following sections incorporate these type questions for you to use during your Bible study discussions.

1 - The Battle Belongs to the Lord

Lesson Scriptures: 1 Samuel 17

Open with prayer

Introduction: Saul's army is facing battle with the Philistines—championed by a giant named Goliath. Goliath taunts the army of God especially its fearful king. David, while on a trip to supply provisions for his brothers, hears the giant rant his defiance of Israel's army, God, and king. In an act of bravery and courage, young David uses his skills, exercises his faith, and then cuts off Goliath's head. Israel defeats the enemy and Saul recognizes David.

Part I – Battle Lines – 1 Samuel 17:1-31
– What did you learn about the Philistine army?
– Why is Saul and the entire army dismayed and terrified?
– How does Saul's stature relate to Goliath's stature (see 1 Samuel 9:2).
– Have you ever been marginalized by someone? How did you feel?...
– What are some ways David's example can inspire a man?

Part II – Battle Courage – 1 Samuel 17:32-39
– What are the attributes of courage that David displays in this situation?
– Why could Saul tell David how to have victory but not be a warrior himself?
– How does the paw of an animal relate to the hand of a giant? (vs 37)
– What experiences in life has God sovereignly provided so you can face life's giants?
– What are ways men becomes fearful and rendered useless in battle?

Part III – Battle Tactics – 1 Samuel 17:40-58
- What are the conditions surrounding the battle between David and Goliath?
- Why did David pick up five stones?
- How does the God of Israel and the God of the Philistines relate together in the minds of each army? (See Kings 20:23.)
- Can you identify a time in your life when you wanted to challenge someone because they dishonored the Name of the Lord?
- What are some ways men can learn to depend on God and then act with bravery?

Review memory verse: 1 Samuel 17:47

Conclusion: While this warfare on earth was between a young man and warrior giant, the real battle was between the God of Israel and the pagan god of the Philistines. Throughout the Bible, God moves in dramatic ways to make His sovereign power known both to Israel and to the nations of the world.

Close with prayer

2 - Friendship, Envy, and Jealousy

Lesson Scripture: – 1 Samuel 18-19

Open with prayer

Introduction: As Jonathon and David grow in their friendship, Saul grows in envy and jealousy. In a plot to kill young David, Saul offers his daughters in marriage. Instead of dying, David doubles the needed dowry and foils the plot. Saul's hatred grows while David's fame spreads. Caught in the middle, Jonathon tries to honor his father, and to love David as a brother. After another fit of rage from King Saul, David seeks help from Samuel the prophet. Saul seeks to find and kill David, but in a strange act of God's Spirit, God protects David.

Part I – Growing Friendship – 1 Samuel 18:1-4
   - What are the attributes for two men who become great friends?
   - What does it mean for a man to "love" another man?
   - How does making a covenant relate to loving another man as yourself?
   - What ways can this example help men develop vital deep friendships today?

Part II – Rising Envy and Increasing Glory – 1 Samuel 18:5-30
   - What are the behaviors Saul demonstrates?
   - Why did God send an evil spirit to torment Saul?
   - How does great success relate to having the Spirit of God?
   - What are the keys to being successful in God's kingdom?
   - You may have had a friend like this in the past but do you presently have a 'friend who sticks closer than a brother'? if so, who is he? If not, are there any potential close friends out there?

Part III – Reconciling Relationships – 1 Samuel 19:1-10
- What sort of behaviors is Saul displaying?
- How do you think Jonathon felt having his father at odds with his best friend?
- How does Saul's behavior compare to his son and daughter?
- What are ways men involve others in ways to disrupt God's work?

Part IV – Surviving Hatred – 1 Samuel 19:11-24
- What did you learn about Saul, David, and Michal in this section?
- Why were idols in David's home and in the care of his wife?
- How did Saul's prophecies relate to the ones he gave in 1 Samuel 10:1-12.
- What are the implications for us as men today?

Review memory verse: Psalm 59:1-2

Conclusion: Eventually, every disciple faces having to choose a course of action because two people closely related to him make opposing demands. When obedience to parents becomes opposed to the bonds of love and friendship, one relationship must be sacrificed for the other. In a similar way, when obedience to God becomes opposed to the bonds of love and friendship with others, the relationship with Christ must take precedence.

Close with prayer

3- Trusting Self

Lesson Scripture: 1 Samuel 21

Open with prayer

Introduction: Up to now, David has done nothing wrong. In fact, he has been a model of a good man humble, faithful, and honest. Suddenly, God puts his faith to the test. His life is in danger; his best friend is forced to choose between friendship and obedience to his father, and his wife acts to honor her father while saving her husband. Like so many men today, David reacts to the situation by taking things into his own hands. His actions and words bring about dire results for others.

Part I – Lies to Ahimelech – 1 Samuel 21:1-9
  - What did you learn about David from this section?
  - Why was the priest concerned about David being alone? (vs 1)
  - Why did he lie to the senior priest?
  - How does this eating of bread relate to Matthew 12:3-4?
  - What is the significance for David in possessing Goliath's sword?
  - How can men today avoid losing their faith and courage in the midst of adversity?

Part II – Lies to Achish – 1 Samuel 21:10-15
  - What events happen in this section?
  - Why did David pretend to be insane?
  - What difference did that make?
  - How does a man's faith in God express itself in his behavior?
  - Who is Doeg?
  - How can men know the difference between a David and a Doeg?

Review memory verse: Psalm 34:9-10

Conclusion: God clearly wants His men to lean on Him. If a man is too dependent on family, friends, or his talents, God will take him through a set of circumstance that result in removing a crutch. Taking things into our own hands and telling lies to protect ourselves is not leaning on God. He is the only source of faith and salvation from our troubles in life.

Close with prayer

4 - Turmoil and Tragedy

Lesson Scripture – 1 Samuel 22

Open with prayer

Introduction: Filled with despair, David finds refuge in the cave at Adullam. Here, he begins to seek out the help of God and the comfort of family and friends. No doubt, his aging parents were not able to keep pace with him and his men. After finding refuge for his parents in the land of their ancestry, he continues to stay on the move. Meanwhile, Saul, filled with murderous hatred, commands the genocide of eighty-five men of God, their families, and livestock.

Part I – The Cave – 1 Samuel 22:1-5
- What lessons did David learn while in cave at Addullam?
- Why did he need to find refuge for his parents?
- What are the kind of men David is collecting for his small army?
- In what way does this relate to men of today who need Christ?

Part II – The Consequence – 1 Samuel 22:6-19
- What are the consequences for assisting David?
- Why did Saul want to have all the priests killed?
- How does this relate to 1 Samuel 2:31-36?
- How can you avoid being part of an evil situation?

Part III – The Concern – 1 Samuel 22:20-23
- What happens in this section?
- Why was Saul unwilling to kill the Amalekites (ch 15), and so willing to kill innocent priests?
- How does this set of adverse circumstances relate to living out God's will?
- In what way is God preparing you or some of the men around you for the future?

Review memory verse: Psalm 142:1-2

Conclusion: Part of David's preparation to reign is seeking and trusting in the leadership and care of God. God wants His men to trust fully in His sovereign control. He often takes men through great periods of turmoil and tragedy in preparation for their future. David's response is captured in Psalm 52 and 142.

Close with prayer

5 – The Presence and Providence of God

Lesson Scriptures: Psalm 139

Open with prayer

Introduction: David wrote this psalm of praise to God for His knowledge of all things, His presence throughout the universe, and His foresight over the earth. He understood that God wants all of His people to fear acts of sin, walk in holiness, and live as intentional believers. In His care and concern for His people, God knows everything and still loves those who are children in His family. The Psalm begins and ends with a prayerful request for God to search David's heart. This is a great example for all of us to follow.

Part I – God's Knowledge 1-6
- What did you learn regarding the knowledge of God?
- How well does God know our thought life?
- Why should that impact the way we behave?
- What are some ways a man can change the way he thinks?

Part II – God's Presence 7-12
- What did you learn about the omnipresence of God?
- Why is it important for men to know God's presence is everywhere?
- How does this section of Scripture relate to Proverbs 15:11
- In what ways should knowing God is present impact a man's actions?

Part III – God's Providence 13-18
- What is God's perspective of the people He creates?
- How does the Psalmist respond to this knowledge?
- Is the book of God filled with foreknowledge or predestination?
- Why should men value the thoughts of God?

Part IV – God's Protection 19-24
- What is David's prayer regarding evil and wicked men?
- Is this OK for us to pray as 21st century Christians? Why or why not?
- What are some good and not so good reasons to pray Psalm 139:23-24?

Review memory verse: Psalm 139:7-10

Conclusion: Men have a tendency to behave one way in a group but another way when they are alone. Almost all the great sins in a man's life are committed when he isolates himself. This is especially compounded when he is alone and dwells in spiritual darkness. Unfortunately, it is easier to dive into the pleasures of sin than it is to pursue sensing His presence and seeking first His righteousness. The more time you spend in His presence getting to know Him, the stronger you become; the stronger you become, the more of His light shines in your life.

Close with prayer

6 – The Danger of Lust

Lesson Scriptures: 2 Samuel 11:1-27

Open with prayer

Introduction: When David should have been on the battlefield, he is lying in bed and indulging his flesh. Looking out from his rooftop, he finds the beauty of a bathing woman and gives in to his lust. Not only does he yield to his lust, he carries his sin further by trying to cover up his actions through manipulation, alcohol, and murder. If David could have foreseen the outcome of his actions, he would have done a much better job of guarding his heart. The Bible states the facts and draws out lessons from the lives of God's men for both good and bad.

Part I: Lust and Sexual Sin – 2 Samuel 11:1-5
   - What is the scenario for David in this section of Scripture?
   - Why should he have been at war instead of home resting?
   - How does this section of Scripture relate to Christ's words in Matthew 5:28?
   - What are ways we can help stay out of lustful situations?

Part II: Manipulation and Control – 2 Samuel 11:6-13
   - What are the lessons you learned in this section?
   - Why was Uriah so dedicated to his brothers in arms?
   - How does this relate to spiritual wars?
   - What can you do to keep from manipulating others?

Part III: Manipulation and Conspiracy – 2 Samuel 11:14-27
- – What are your observations in these verses?
- – Why did Joab want the messenger to be sure to mention the death of Uriah?
- – How does David's flippant response to Uriah's death (11:25) relate to his response over Saul or Abner's death? (2 Samuel 1:11-27; 3:31-39)
- – What applications can you make from this aspect of David's example?

Review memory verse: 2 Samuel 11:11

Conclusion: David was careless in allowing his eyes to wander and then yield to the lust of his flesh. All men must learn to control the lust of the flesh, lust of the eyes, and the boastful pride of life. Otherwise, their evil wants drag them away into a world of enticement. After a desire is ill conceived, it gives birth to sin; and sin, when it is full-grown, gives birth to death. (James 1:14-15)

Close with prayer

7. Final Words and Faithful Friends

Lesson Scriptures: 2 Samuel 23:1-39

Open with prayer

Introduction: This study contains two sections. In the first section David speaks about leading men, and in the second is a list of the mighty men he led. In the process of leading and loving those around him, David develops strong bonds with this band of brothers who were mighty in deeds and loyal in their friendship. These men were loyal to David because he was loyal to them. If you want to know what kind of person a leader is, look at the kind of people that they lead.

Part I: Final Words – 2 Samuel 23:1-7
- What kind of inspiration did these words give you?
- Since this is a prophetic Psalm, who is David referring to? (v 3)
- How does the Holy Spirit inspire you?
- What kind of words would you like to record as your last on this earth?
- What are some ways men can improve the way God leads them at home?

    At work?
    At church?
    In the community?

Part II: Faithful Friends – 2 Samuel 23:8-39
- Which one of these men inspires you the most? Why?
- What were these men like in the beginning?
  (See 1 Samuel 22:2.)
- What were you like in the beginning of your spiritual life?
- Why did David pour out the water as an offering rather than quench his thirst?
- How was David a good leader of these men?
- How was he a poor leader of these men?
- What can you do to improve the way you lead others?
- At home, work, church, and community?

Review memory verse: 2 Samuel 23:2-4

Conclusion: David was an outstanding leader when he was devoted to following His Leader. Devotion requires routine contact and submission. As we meet with God, we can depend on Him for help and guidance. This fuels good leading and loving. Godly men who lead at home, at work, and in the community give life to others just like God gives life to them. As they live and love the people in their sphere of influence, their impact grows.

Close with prayer

8. On Your Death Bed

Lesson Scriptures: 1 Kings 1:1-2:18

Open with prayer

Introduction: As David approaches seventy years of age, his body is weak and perhaps diseased. Adonijah sees this situation and attempts to set himself up as king. Sensing his inability to deal with more rebellions and to lead the kingdom, David declares Solomon as the next ruler of Israel. In a short but classic set of Scriptures, David the father issues Solomon the son a charge to be strong and show himself a man by keeping the commandments of the Lord.

Part I: The Upward Rebellion – 2 Kings 1:1-27
- What is David's physical and perhaps mental condition at this point in his life?
- How does this factor into Adonijah's actions and decisions to make himself king?
- Why is loyalty then and now so important for men especially leaders?
- How do you think David felt knowing Abiathar sided with Adonijah? (1 Sam 22:20)
- Once again, Nathan the prophet helps the king. What is significant about his actions?
- What are some ways you can apply this section of Scripture to your life?

Part II: The Ultimate Ruler – 2 Kings 1:27-53
- What did you learn from this section of Scripture?
- How did David ensure a smooth transition of leadership? (28-40)
- Why was it important to anoint Solomon with oil? (38-39)
- What are some ways you can help others be more secure in their leadership?

Part III: The Ultra Challenge – 2 Kings 2:1-12
- – How are both young men and old men behaving in our modern world?
- – What is unique about David's challenge to his son?
- – Why is it critical for men to grow up and be godly at home, at work, and in the church?
- – What are some things you would like to say to your son in a similar situation?

Review memory verse: 2 Kings 2:2-3

Conclusion: Like David to Solomon, all men should encourage and warn their sons be strong and to act like men. David gave sound advice to his son. It would be up to Solomon to follow it or not. All men need to use their strength and masculinity for the good of others. All men need to keep God the center of their personal and public life.

Close with prayer

BIBLE STUDY AGREEMENT

I, _____, agree with my men's study group to do the following:

1. Complete the Bible study for each week before the muster session.

2. Bring my Bible, completed Bible study, a pen/pencil and paper to the muster sessions.

3. Take part in all muster sessions unless urgent circumstances beyond my control prevent attendance. When unable to attend, I will make up the session at the earliest possible time with a team leader or team member.

4. Share openly and honestly in the muster sessions.

5. Pray regularly for my band of brothers.

6. Keep confidential any personal matters shared by others in the team.

7. Pray at least weekly for my senior and associate pastor(s).

8. Not manipulate or pressure others to do what I think is best. I will simply bear witness to what I sense God may be saying to this band of brothers and watch and see how His Spirit leads.

Please pray over the contents of this agreement before signing. Once you are convinced this is a calling from God, sign the document and give it to your Bible study leader.

Signature: _____Date: _____

ABOUT THE AUTHORS

Brad Stewart and Brian Doyle

B rad Stewart is the President of Kingdom Warrior. Before starting this ministry, he served as the director of men's ministry in his home church and throughout the Pacific Northwest for his denomination. While formerly in the U.S. military, Brad performed as Vice Chairman of the Board of Directors for the Yokosuka Japan Christian Serviceman's Center, and spent fifteen years making disciples while laboring in the Navigators. He is a retired U.S. Navy Senior Chief Petty Officer. He holds a B.S. from Excelsior College, Albany, New York, and an M.T.S. and D.Min. from Columbia Evangelical Seminary (CES), Buckley, Washington. In addition, Brad serves as an advisory member on the CES board of regents. He lives in Washington State with his wife Barbra. Together, they work to advance the Kingdom of God. You can learn more about Kingdom Warrior at www.KingdomWarrior.net or contact Brad directly at nwbattlecry@gmail.com.

For future Kingdom Warrior Bible Studies and Men's Ministry related materials, be sure to view www.KingdomWarrior.net/tools

Brian Doyle is passionate to see churches equip men for spiritual leadership in the home, church and community. He has served with The Navigators on campuses and military bases, as well as on staff with Promise Keepers in the 1990's. Brian now serves as Founder and

President of Iron Sharpens Iron, which equips churches to train men for spiritual leadership. He oversees the Iron Sharpens Iron Conference Network which hosts equipping conferences for men around the nation. These conferences are the most visible part of the regional ministries that equip churches to reach and build godly men. Brian also serves on the Board of Directors of The Fatherhood Commission and on the Executive Board of the National Coalition of Men's Ministries. He and his wife, Barbara, consider it a privilege to model and disciple their five children to follow Jesus Christ. You can learn more about Iron Sharpens Iron at www.IronSharpensIron.net or contact him at brian.doyle@ IronSharpensIron.net.

For future Iron Sharpens Iron Bible Studies and Men's Ministry related materials, be sure to view www.IronSharpensIron.net/ resources.

ENDNOTES

1   Hughes, R. B., & Laney, J. C. (2001). *Tyndale concise Bible commentary* (p. 110). Wheaton, IL: Tyndale House Publishers.

2   (2014-02-01). 1 and 2 Samuel (LifeChange) (Kindle Locations 980-981). NavPress. Kindle Edition.

3   (2014-02-01). 1 and 2 Samuel (LifeChange) (Kindle Locations 980-981). NavPress. Kindle Edition.

4   Elwell, W.A., & Comfort, P.W. (2001). In *Tyndale Bible dictionary*. Wheaton, IL: Tyndale House Publishers.

5   Henry, M. (1994). *Matthew Henry's commentary on the whole Bible: complete and unabridged in one volume* (p. 418). Peabody: Hendrickson.

6   (2014-02-01). 1 and 2 Samuel (LifeChange) (Kindle Locations 1154-1158). NavPress. Kindle Edition.

7   Elwell, W. A., & Comfort, P.W. (2001). In *Tyndale Bible dictionary*. Wheaton, IL: Tyndale House Publishers.

8   Easton, M. G. (1893). In *Easton's Bible dictionary*. New York: Harper & Brothers.

9   International Standard Bible Encyclopedia

10 (2000). The Application Study Bible, Grand Rapids, MI.: Zondervan

11 (2000). The Application Study Bible, Grand Rapids, MI.: Zondervan

12 Elwell, W.A., & Comfort, P.W. (2001). In *Tyndale Bible dictionary*. Wheaton, IL: Tyndale House Publishers.

13 (2014-02-01). 1 and 2 Samuel (LifeChange) (Kindle Locations 2805-2807). NavPress. Kindle Edition.

14 Baldwin, J.G. (1988). *1 and 2 Samuel: An Introduction and Commentary* (Vol. 8, pp. 314–315). Downers Grove, IL: InterVarsity Press.

15 Wiseman, D.J. (1993). *1 and 2 Kings: an introduction and commentary* (Vol. 9, p. 78). Downers Grove, IL: InterVarsity Press.

16 Freeman, J.M., & Chadwick, H.J. (1998). *Manners & customs of the Bible* (p. 233). North Brunswick, NJ: Bridge-Logos Publishers.

17 Patterson, R.D., & Austel, H.J. (1988). 1, 2 Kings. In F.E.Gaebelein (Ed.), *The Expositor's Bible Commentary: 1 & 2 Kings, 1 & 2 Chronicles, Ezra, Nehemiah, Esther, Job* (Vol. 4, p. 34). Grand Rapids, MI: Zondervan Publishing House.

CPSIA information can be obtained
at www.ICGtesting.com
Printed in the USA
FFOW03n1619120217
32213FF